The City *of*

SAN DIEGO

SAN DIEGO PUBLIC LIBRARY

In honor of our dear friend

Ceci Russell,

who loved life,

nature, & the magic of books!

TAKING ACTION TO HELP THE ENVIRONMENT

ERIC BRAUN

Lerner Publications ◆ Minneapolis

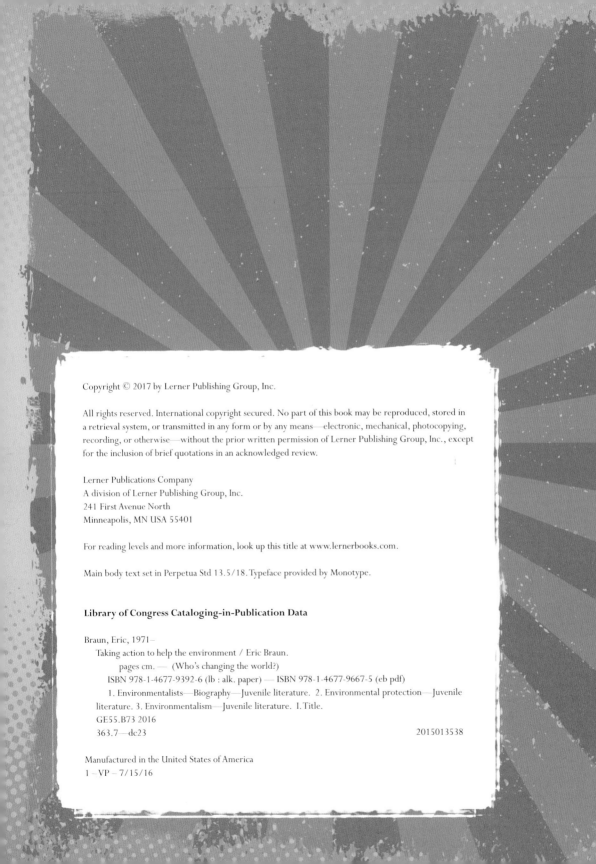

Lerner Publications Company
A division of Lerner Publishing Group, Inc.
241 First Avenue North
Minneapolis, MN USA 55401

For reading levels and more information, look up this title at www.lernerbooks.com.

Main body text set in Perpetua Std 13.5/18. Typeface provided by Monotype.

Library of Congress Cataloging-in-Publication Data

Braun, Eric, 1971–
    Taking action to help the environment / Eric Braun.
        pages cm. — (Who's changing the world?)
    ISBN 978-1-4677-9392-6 (lb : alk. paper) — ISBN 978-1-4677-9667-5 (eb pdf)
    1. Environmentalists—Biography—Juvenile literature. 2. Environmental protection—Juvenile literature. 3. Environmentalism—Juvenile literature. I. Title.
    GE55.B73 2016
    363.7—dc23   2015013538

Manufactured in the United States of America
1 – VP – 7/15/16

CONTENTS

INTRODUCTION
ENVIRONMENTAL ACTIVISM

Some environmental activists plan or attend rallies and protests.

Tens of thousands of people march in New York City to raise awareness of global warming. A nun chains herself to the gate of a factory to draw attention to air pollution. An actor speaks to Congress about endangered animals. A fifth grader in North Carolina writes to his mayor to ask her to vote on an organic farming bill. These people are all environmental activists.

They each noticed a problem, and they took action. Whether the problem that attracted their attention was related to food, climate change, or another environmental issue, they all became activists because they wanted to make a change in their world.

It's easy to feel overwhelmed when you think about our environment. Animals are going extinct. Coal, oil, and other fossil fuels are polluting the air. Climate change is threatening human, animal,

Factories and power plants can release pollutants into the air. Concerned people might find a way to take action.

and plant life. The food people eat might be chock-full of unknown ingredients. It can be enough to make you grab the TV remote and settle in for your favorite escape.

Or you can decide to do something about an issue you care about. You don't have to be a member of Congress or a famous entertainer or even live in a big city. You don't have to be old enough to vote or get a job. You don't even have to be old enough to read to be an activist! You just need to have the desire to make a change and the commitment to follow through on an action.

CHAPTER 1
PROTECTING ANIMALS

Olivia Bouler in 2012

OLIVIA BOULER
SAVING BIRDS THROUGH ART

Olivia Bouler was an eleven-year-old artist and bird lover when the Deepwater Horizon oil rig exploded and sank off the coast of Louisiana in April 2010. Within months, the sinking ship spilled nearly 5 million gallons (18.9 million liters) of oil into the Gulf of Mexico. It was the world's largest-ever marine oil spill.

Olivia watched as people from across the United States joined a rescue and cleanup effort. The goal was to contain the spreading oil and protect wildlife from its harmful effects. But Olivia was focused on one particular impact of the oil: its effect on birds.

Olivia learned that birds can't avoid oil as it spreads in water. They need to dive into the water to find fish to eat. But when they get oil on their feathers, birds can lose their ability to fly. They also swallow oil as they dive and eat. And that's poisonous for them.

Although she lived more than 1,000 miles (1,609 kilometers) away, in Long Island, New York, Olivia had spent summers with family in Louisiana. She loved the many birds living near the Gulf of Mexico. And she knew she wanted to do something to help save them.

Olivia had always admired the naturalist and artist James Audubon, who painted and described the birds of North America in his book *Birds*

A brown pelican covered in oil from the Deepwater Horizon oil spill in 2010

of America. And she knew the nonprofit National Audubon Society, named after Audubon, worked to protect birds and other wildlife from environmental damage. After the Deepwater spill, the Audubon Society started raising money to help clean up the Gulf and protect the birds there.

Olivia decided to help the Audubon Society in whatever way she could. But as a kid, what could she offer? She didn't have a lot of money. She did have a skill, though: drawing. She wrote the Audubon Society a letter and offered to make original drawings of birds for each person who donated money to help birds. "Eleven years old and willing to help," she wrote.

The Audubon Society took her up on her offer. Olivia drew and donated five hundred drawings. AOL helped out by donating $25,000, hosting her drawings on its website, and distributing thousands of prints.

Olivia's drawings helped raise more than $200,000 for Gulf recovery efforts. The Audubon Society named her the 2011 Artist Inspiring Conservation.

Recognition for Olivia's efforts didn't stop there. She went to Washington, DC, to visit members of Congress. Her local House representative, Steve Israel, named her a Hometown Hero. She was even honored by the White House, who named her a Champion of Change. She became the only kid among fourteen people honored as Service and Social Innovators.

Olivia was also named a Disney Friend for Change and a Dale Earnhardt Legend of Leadership. In addition, she won the 2010 ASPCA Tommy P. Monahan Kid of the Year Award, named in honor of a Staten Island boy who died in 2007 while trying to save his pet from a house fire.

Following in the footsteps of her hero James Audubon, Olivia published her own book about birds. *Olivia's Birds: Saving the Gulf* was published on the one-year anniversary of the Deepwater spill. It features

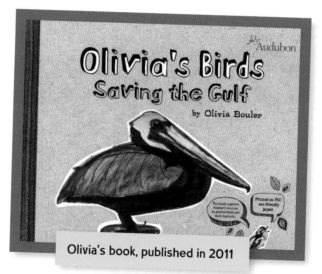

Olivia's book, published in 2011

her original drawings along with photos of many different birds. She donated proceeds from the book to further help Gulf cleanup efforts.

As she gets older, Olivia continues her activism to help birds. She has traveled throughout the world to share her love of birds and help spread awareness about the dangers faced by birds and other wildlife.

ELLA VAN CLEAVE
REDUCING DOLPHIN HUNTING

Ella Van Cleave is proud to be a teenage activist, but she says nobody was as surprised as she was to find herself wearing that label. "When I was a bit younger I would hear the word 'activist' and immediately my mind would wander to these images of highly opinionated people taking their beliefs to the streets with signs and megaphones—and I couldn't help but just sit there and think, *What are these people doing?*"

When Ella learned how poorly some dolphins near Japan were treated, she wanted to help them.

Flash-forward to the summer Ella was twelve. A friend introduced her to a movie about one of her favorite topics: dolphins. Only the movie wasn't about how adorable or fascinating dolphins are. It was about the yearly slaughter of thousands of dolphins in the Japanese community of Taiji. Ella later said that movie—the Oscar-winning documentary *The Cove*—was the thing that "opened the floodgates" of activism for her.

The Cove highlights a practice known as dolphin drive hunting, in which dolphins are herded into a cove near Taiji. Once captured in the cove, some of the dolphins are sold to aquariums and marine parks around the world. The rest of the dolphins—several thousand each year, according to the film—are slaughtered with spears and knives. Their meat is sold to food companies.

After viewing this treatment of dolphins, Ella realized she wanted to do what she could to change those practices. And she wanted to protect not just dolphins but sharks and other wildlife that were hunted by humans. She said the film opened her eyes to a whole world of animal mistreatment. "I was introduced to a world where sharks were bludgeoned and murdered for their fins," she said.

And so the twelve-year-old from Chattanooga, Tennessee, became an activist. "From there, you start to become aware that the particular issue you're advocating for is just a small piece of the puzzle, and once you get a glimpse of the larger picture you've seen enough to know that you can't just stop there, and that there will be a lifetime of work in all sorts of different issues ahead of you," Ella said.

Ella started an online petition to save dolphins. She began giving speeches throughout the United States. When her family moved to

People protest the killing of dolphins in Taiji, Japan.

Canada, she gave speeches there too. She spoke at universities and large events. In January 2012, at the age of fourteen, she presented a TEDxYouth talk in Victoria, Canada, about the plight of the dolphins. She said the goal of her speeches was to help persuade people to pay attention to what was happening to ocean wildlife.

Later in 2012, Ella made her own video showing graphic scenes of dolphin slaughter. It included her own footage, as well as scenes shot by other conservationists. Ella entered the video in a contest by One World One Ocean, an ocean conservation group and film studio. She won the contest and was invited to join Mission Aquarius in the Florida Keys. Mission Aquarius was a six-day underwater journey to the world's only remaining undersea laboratory, Aquarius Reef Base. The mission's purpose was to raise awareness for the research being done at the lab. As part of the project, Ella got to meet one of her heroes, the oceanographer Sylvia Earle.

When Ella won a video contest, her prize was to spend six days visiting the Aquarius Reef Base laboratory in Florida.

Ella didn't slow down as an activist as she got older. In high school, she became involved in activism addressing the issues of overpopulation and climate change.

JANE GOODALL
STUDYING CHIMPS AND PRESERVING WILDLIFE

Jane Goodall is considered the world authority on chimpanzees. She's credited with inspiring tens of thousands of young people to study science. She has movies, books, and even a scientific institute named after her. But for the last several decades, Goodall has focused her efforts on protecting chimps and other wildlife from environmental harm. *TakePart* magazine called her "the world's most influential animal activist."

Jane Goodall with Mr. H, her stuffed monkey, in 2011.

Born in England in 1934, Jane Goodall was fascinated with animals from a young age. She spent much of her childhood free time watching and drawing animals. She described one of her earliest memories: "One of my earliest recollections is of the day that I hid in a small stuffy henhouse in order to see how a hen laid an egg. I emerged after about five hours. The whole household had apparently been searching for me for hours, and mother had even rung the police to report me missing." Meanwhile, Goodall dreamed about going to Africa to see animals in their natural habitats. Her dream came true at the age of twenty-three, when she traveled to Tanzania to be a secretary for a chimpanzee researcher. After that, she was hooked. Goodall has spent nearly six decades observing, learning about, and describing chimp behavior.

By spending time living with chimpanzees in their natural environment, Goodall was able to see more of their natural behavior than many researchers had been able to. Her discoveries helped document many similarities between humans and other primates. The more she learned about chimps, the fonder she grew of them.

In 1986, after she went to a conference on chimpanzees in Chicago, Goodall became a serious supporter of wildlife preservation. At the conference, she learned about the chimpanzee's endangered habitat. She also realized many chimps were mistreated as subjects of scientific research. She decided to focus her efforts on raising public awareness for these issues. She had already started a chimp research group called the Jane Goodall Institute in 1977. Soon the institute was focusing on chimp protection as much as chimp research. And in 1991, she added a youth program called Roots & Shoots. The program's goal is to encourage youth to identify issues in their communities, make plans for change, and take action for change. It began with a group of twelve teenagers from Tanzania who wanted to make a difference. Any group that focuses on people, animals, or the environment can be part of Goodall's program.

Goodall with one of her research subjects in the Gombe Stream National Park in northern Tanzania in 1972

Goodall *(left)* and other members of Roots & Shoots lead an International Day of Peace demonstration in New York City in 2009.

The year after forming Roots & Shoots, Goodall had an experience that made her expand her focus from protecting chimps to protecting all living things, including plants, animals, and people. She was flying in a small plane around a national park in Tanzania when she saw that the land was in worse shape than she had imagined. "I knew there was deforestation out of the park, but I had no idea it was almost total," she said. "It was a shock. It was bare, bare, bare hills." She had long known that forest destruction was hurting the chimpanzees. But now she also saw the extent of poverty and violence—from a civil war—that humans in the region were suffering from. "How could we protect these famous chimpanzees when the people were living in these terrible situations?" she asked. It was then that she decided to dedicate time to improving life not just for wildlife but for humans too.

Goodall continued traveling, speaking, and raising awareness of the issues of environmental damage and poverty. As she met more young people through Roots & Shoots, she realized many felt let down by older generations. They also felt powerless to do anything about it. Roots & Shoots aims to give them power to change the world. It has grown into a global network with 150,000 members in more than 130 countries, working on local and global service projects. Projects include work on issues such as hunger, pollution, and animal welfare.

CHAPTER 2
SLOWING CLIMATE CHANGE

Alec Loorz speaks at a rally in Los Angeles in 2010.

ALEC LOORZ
RAISING AWARENESS IN KIDS

Alec Loorz can pinpoint exactly when he realized he wanted to become a climate change activist. It was 2006, and Alec was twelve years old, when he saw the film *An Inconvenient Truth*. The movie follows former vice president Al Gore's efforts to educate the public on global warming. In the film, which won an Academy Award, Gore describes the impacts on Earth that he and many scientists believe will occur if humans don't change their habits. "After I saw *An Inconvenient Truth*," Alec remembered, "I was freaked out about what was happening . . . and was infuriated that there were people who were preventing action."

Alec said when he started spreading the word about the threat of global warming, a lot of people didn't believe him. He realized he wanted to know more than he had learned from *An Inconvenient Truth*. He applied to be trained as a presenter by Al Gore and the

Climate Change Project, but he was told he was too young. So Alec began researching scientific papers he found online. He became more convinced that the threat was huge—and more convinced that he wanted to raise awareness of the issue. He even met with scientists who did research on the subject and with politicians. He learned it would be hard to bring change because fossil fuel companies spent so much money to keep things the same.

When he was thirteen, Alec started his own organization, Kids vs. Global Warming. Its goal was to inspire and help other young people to speak out about global warming. The first project he organized was called SLAP, the Sea Level Awareness Project. "It bothered me that nobody in my coastal town of Ventura, California, was really paying attention to the threats of climate change," he said. "I came up with a way to make it more visible to people: a series of nine-foot [2.7-meter] poles along the coastline that shows people that we will be underwater if we do nothing

Al Gore (left) talks with Alec Loorz about his Climate Change Project presentation in 2009.

AN INCONVENIENT TRUTH

Al Gore turned environmental activism into a second career. As a politician, Gore had long been a champion of environmental policy. But after he lost the 2000 presidential election to George W. Bush, he turned his attention full-time to issues related to climate change. He traveled around the United States and the rest of the world giving presentations on global warming. His presentation was featured in the 2006 Academy Award-winning documentary *An Inconvenient Truth*. The following year, Gore shared the Nobel Peace Prize with the Intergovernmental Panel on Climate Change. In 2010 Gore started a new group called the Climate Reality Project, which aims to raise awareness of climate change and empower people to make a difference in fighting global warming. The group's website says,

> Whether it's watching a video that helps build your awareness, sharing a post with your friends and family, signing a petition against Big Polluters, or organizing a climate presentation in your community, your actions will take this movement forward. We can create a better future, but only if we do it together.

about the climate crisis." Alec worked with a group of about fifty of his fellow middle schoolers to design and install the poles along the beach. They even met with the City of Ventura to get its cooperation.

Alec started giving presentations to youth around the country. He included video and animation to make his points about the research he had done. He spoke to kids from kindergarten all the way to college. Once he had made about thirty presentations, he received exciting news. He had been invited to be trained by Al Gore. He went to the training, and at the age of fourteen, he became the Climate Project's youngest trained presenter in the country.

In 2007, Alec launched the iMatter initiative of Kids vs. Global Warming, to provide more opportunities for young people's voices to be heard. iMatter helps young people participate in activities including community projects like Alec's original SLAP, public speaking, and legal actions.

ANNA ROSE MOHR-ALMEIDA
HELPING ENDANGERED ANIMALS

It was a Michael Jackson video she saw at the age of eleven that first inspired Anna Mohr-Almeida to become an activist. At first, she was most passionate about animal rights. The video, "Earth Song," showed elephants who were killed for their tusks. Anna said learning about that needless slaughter made her sad.

Soon, Anna became concerned about other animals that were in danger of going extinct. She wanted to do something about it. As she explained, "I became attached to pandas and was worried they would become extinct." Anna started

Anna Rose Mohr-Almeida addresses the Arizona Corporation Commission in 2013.

making jewelry at school out of recycled materials. She sold it, and in about three months, she had made $85, which she gave to an animal sanctuary in Utah.

Anna, who lives in Mesa, Arizona, said once she became active in animal rights, it didn't take her long to realize that climate change was to blame for a lot of the issues animals are facing. Anna started a youth council that lets her work with other kids taking action and speaking out about climate change. She says she loves working with her fellow council members because it's fun to hang out together doing projects in the community— and they often go out for ice cream when their work is done.

To help her raise money to fight climate change and other issues, Anna also founded her own nonprofit called Kids Climate Action Network (Kids CAN). Kids CAN aims to help young people participate in efforts to reduce climate change, improve human health, support animal rights, and fight for other causes. She also continues to participate in marches and speak out about climate change. In fifth grade, she spoke out against coal plants in front of the Arizona Corporation Commission. She asked the commission's members to think about the polar bears and the people who get sick from breathing dirty air. She asked them to stop polluting and to support renewable energy.

Then Anna was invited to speak about climate change at other important meetings and events.

WORRIED ABOUT THE FUTURE

"I'm really worried about the future. Climate change is happening. Ice caps are melting, animals are becoming extinct faster than ever before, and trees are being cut down to make way for factory farming. Our governments, which are supposed to protect the people, instead pave the way for activities that destroy the Earth, and along with it, my future."

–Anna Mohr-Almeida

She said her goal is to get people to "stop pretending that everything is normal and fine." She spoke to the US Environmental Protection

Agency (EPA) at a clean air hearing, and she spoke to the Arizona Corporation Commission in support of renewable energy. "Sharing my concerns at rallies and demonstrations really made an impact, and it felt great!" she said. "The next thing I knew, my family and I were marching in the New York City climate march, which was an amazing experience."

Thousands of demonstrators of all ages participated in the People's Climate March in New York City on September 21, 2014.

In March 2015, she was named Member of the Month by the iMatter Campaign—founded by fellow climate change activist Alec Loorz. At the time, she was planning to join a protest at an event called Funeral for Solar in Tempe, Arizona. "My youth council and I are going to lay on the ground in body bags to show people how many deaths in Arizona are connected to burning coal for energy," she said.

KATHY JETNIL-KIJINER
CREATING SPOKEN-WORD POETRY

Poet and spoken-word artist Kathy Jetnil-Kijiner had her largest audience ever when she spoke at the opening ceremony of the United Nations Climate Summit in September 2014. Jetnil-Kijiner, who is from the Marshall Islands in the northern Pacific Ocean, said she was thrilled to get a chance to speak to world leaders. "I want to bring my people's message out to the world, that climate change is a threat we need to take more seriously," she said.

Kathy Jetnil-Kijiner speaks at the United Nations Climate Change Summit in 2014.

Jetnil-Kijiner has been a poet longer than she's been an activist. As she explains, "I was writing poetry from third grade—my first poem was about an invisible elephant! But I didn't take it seriously until my senior year, when we had two substitute teachers in my English class. They were spoken-word artists and it was the first time that I'd heard that style. For some reason, it just clicked and I loved it straight away."

But her writing has always had an activism angle. While climate change is one of the biggest issues she addresses, she focuses on raising awareness for many challenges that face her people on the Marshall Islands. The Marshall Islands is a small country with close ties to the United States. It has fewer than seventy thousand people spread out over many small islands near the equator in the Pacific Ocean. One of the issues facing Marshallese people that Jetnil-Kijiner writes about is how climate change has led the sea level to rise in the Marshall Islands. It threatens to ruin homes and even overtake some of the islands entirely.

Another issue Jetnil-Kijiner writes and speaks out about is the effects of nuclear testing that has been conducted on the islands.

After World War II (1939–1945), the United States tested sixty-seven nuclear weapons in the Marshall Islands. Since then the nuclear fallout has caused thousands of residents to suffer serious health issues.

After attending college in California and graduate school in Hawaii, Jetnil-Kijiner returned to the Marshall Islands and began teaching, writing, and performing poetry. She became an activist when she started getting invitations to read her poetry about climate change, nuclear testing, and other issues. Because youth in Pacific Island cultures are typically expected not to be outspoken, Jetnil-Kijiner has said she sometimes faces criticism. "I definitely feel pressure at home, where Marshallese girls are quiet and nice," she explains. "However when you look at our past, when you look at our culture, it's actually rooted in women who were really powerful, women who speak out."

The Marshall Islands, home of Kathy Jetnil-Kijiner

Jetnil-Kijiner lives in the Marshall Islands with her daughter. Along with writing, she loves to perform. She hosts open mic events, competes in slam poetry competitions, and performs at showcases and conferences.

CHAPTER 3
PROMOTING CLEAN ENERGY

Xiuhtezcatl Roske-Martinez in 2014

XIUHTEZCATL ROSKE-MARTINEZ
HONORING HIS AZTEC ROOTS

Xiuhtezcatl Roske-Martinez gave his first speech at a climate change rally when he was six years old. The Boulder, Colorado, native got his name (pronounced "Shu-TEZ-caht") from Aztec elders of Mexico, who chose it based on the Aztec calendar. Xiuhtezcatl gets his indigenous roots from his father. But he inherited a love of activism from both of his parents, who are environmental activists. "I've always grown up in nature, playing in these lakes and rivers and hiking in mountains," he explains. "My father raised me in the Aztec tradition, so I've always had a connection to nature. He taught me that all life is sacred, and that all life needed to be protected."

When he was still in grade school, Xiuhtezcatl joined the Earth Guardians, a group of young people working to protect the environment that his mother started. Much of his early activism took place in his hometown of Boulder. There he appeared at environmental rallies and in front of the city council. Xiuhtezcatl helped end the city's use of pesticides in its parks. He also fought for a fee on plastic bags to limit their use at stores.

By the time he was twelve, Xiuhtezcatl had organized more than thirty-five rallies and protests. He co-organized an iMatter youth march with more than two thousand participants. In 2012 he was among the 24 Under 24 leaders selected by the Campaign for a Presidential Youth Council. He has advocated for many changes to make the environment safer. He has tried to convince leaders in business and government to replace oil and natural gas with renewable energy sources. He even helped end the city's two-decade agreement with a natural gas company, in favor of using renewable energy. He argues that adults are letting down future generations by caring more about money than the environment. "They care more about money in their pockets than they

Activists Xiuhtezcatl Roske-Martinez and Karen Dike *(right)* present health studies to decision makers in Denver, Colorado, in 2015.

do about the survival of the next generation," he says. "We can't let money and greed and power rule our world anymore."

Xiuhtezcatl later focused his attention on one particularly damaging activity: fracking. Fracking is a way of getting natural gas from deep inside Earth. Natural gas and oil companies fracture shale rocks to release gas. The companies drill and inject fluid into the ground to fracture the rocks. But the fluid they use contains many toxic chemicals. Environmentalists are concerned that this process damages the air and water for miles around the drilling sites. It also takes a lot of water and energy to extract small amounts of gas.

A hip-hop lover, Xiuhtezcatl helped spread the word about the dangers of fracking by performing an anti-fracking song at schools and rallies in Colorado and around the country. "Natural gas isn't the way to go," he sings. "We want to get fracking out of our town." A November 2013 video of him performing the song that he wrote has gotten more than fifteen thousand hits on YouTube.

KIMBERLY WASSERMAN
CLEARING THE AIR

In 1998, when Kimberly Wasserman's son was two months old, she had to rush him to the hospital because he could barely breathe. She learned he had asthma. Then she learned the asthma had been caused, at least in part, by the polluted air in her neighborhood.

Wasserman lived in the Little Village neighborhood of Chicago. Little Village is a mostly Latino neighborhood next door to two of the country's oldest coal-fired power plants. The neighborhood kids called the plants' smokestacks "cloud factories." But really, the plants were blowing pollution and coal dust into the air. The dust landed all over the neighborhood: on houses, schools, and parks.

After Wasserman learned her son had asthma, she found out that many local residents had breathing problems that were most likely caused by the power plants. Wasserman worked for a community agency called the Little Village Environmental Justice Organization. As part of her job, she went door-to-door to survey residents. As she learned more about the pollution, she started asking residents about their experiences.

Kimberly Wasserman in 2013

Wasserman spoke to her neighbors about illnesses in their families. She explained how the power plants were harming residents and causing breathing problems. She convinced neighbors to band together and demand that the company that owned the plants make changes. It was hard work. Many of the residents were new to the United States. Some spoke only Spanish. Some were in the country illegally and didn't want to get involved.

But Wasserman pushed forward. Her group of activists didn't have a lot of money. But by joining together, they were able to make their voices heard. As a Latina, Wasserman knew that she would gain people's trust and their interest by incorporating Latino cultural practices into her work. As she later described, "A lot of what helped us was looking at the history of where our people come from. Taking the lessons

The Little Village Environmental Justice Organization protest in Chicago in 2009

we learned from both Mexican and Mexican-American history, and looking at movement building and murals and art and street theater, and how all of those things played into communication of a struggle and a solution—we tried to incorporate posters and art and murals." Wasserman described one street theater production as "clean power elections," in which wind and solar power candidates stood on one corner while "on the other corner we had coal barons dressed to the nines in tuxedos." Those actions helped explain what was happening in a way that neighbors understood.

The Little Village activists contacted news organizations and picketed in front of the plants. They even organized Toxic Tours that showed the damage the plants were causing. At the time, Chicago was trying to win the honor of holding the 2016 Olympics. So Little Village activists held a Coal Olympics, in which kids jumped over cardboard models of coal plants and mountains destroyed by mining, to further raise awareness of their situation. All these efforts helped lead to the first Chicago Clean Power Coalition in 2011.

Soon Chicago passed a law called the Clean Power Ordinance. The law required power companies to improve their pollution control efforts and reduce the smoke they released. Faced with the expense of making those changes, the power company that owned the plants near Little Village closed both plants in 2012. Wasserman and her fellow activists had succeeded in their mission to improve air quality in their neighborhood. In 2013 she won the North America Goldman Environmental Prize, one of the highest honors for environmental activism.

But Wasserman didn't stop there. She continued to fight for cleaner air. She trained younger people to become activists.

ADVICE TO YOUNG ACTIVISTS

"Definitely don't give up. And definitely arm yourself with as much research as possible. We have to be arming our young people to be thinking about careers in math and science and engineering to be able to bring those skills back and help us tackle some of these environmental-justice issues. When our campaign started, some of our young people were in first or second grade, and those young people are now in college, getting their masters in environmental justice, because this had such a resonating effect on them."

—Kimberly Wasserman

And she worked to transform the former power plants into open spaces for the neighborhood. She wants to build more places where residents can enjoy clean air and get exercise. She wants to see playgrounds, skate parks, and picnic sites. She says her vision for these spaces is to serve as a community "front porch," where people can get together with their neighbors and talk about ways to improve their community.

Vandana Shiva in 2013

VANDANA SHIVA
STANDING UP FOR SMALL-SCALE FARMERS

Vandana Shiva dresses in the traditional saris of her native India. She will turn sixty-five in 2017 and looks like a typical Indian grandmother. But she is not a typical grandmother. She's one of the world's fiercest food activists. Like many, she believes the world will face food shortages in the coming decades. But unlike those who believe large-scale farming is the answer to this problem, Shiva believes that small-scale, organic farming is the solution.

Shiva started out in physics, earning her PhD from the University of Western Ontario in Canada in 1978. But she soon found it more interesting to think about farming than physics. In the 1980s, she attended a conference on the future of food. People at the conference were talking about the need to genetically modify food. It was the beginning of the genetically modified organism (GMO) movement. Scientists at the conference said they needed to genetically modify seeds to make them grow more easily throughout the world. They said they wanted to develop these new types of seeds and take out patents on them.

This idea concerned Shiva. For one thing, seeds and crops are a type of life, and she didn't think a company should be able to get a trademark on a type of life. "I realized they want to patent life, and life is not an invention," she said. But she was also concerned that big businesses wanted to develop these new seeds and crops and then, without testing the effect on humans, start making food from them. Shiva thought that if people began eating this untested food, they might be harmed in unexpected ways. She worried about how this might affect India's small farmers too. She thought they would be driven out of business by the large farms using genetically

A farmer checks on his organic crops in the village of Manpura, India.

modified seeds. Shiva began working to prevent the use of genetically modified seed and large-scale farming.

After that conference, Shiva started an organization called Navdanya, which means "Nine Seeds" in Hindi, her native language.

The group's mission is to protect native (unmodified) seed and to promote organic farming. In the decades since she started the group, Shiva has been hugely successful in raising awareness throughout India—and the rest of the world—about the dangers of large-scale farming and genetically altered seeds. Those dangers as Shiva describes them are that big corporations rely heavily on chemical fertilizers and pesticides, as well as fossil fuels and an enormous amount of water. They also plant huge fields of a single crop. That lack of diversity, along with the use of human-made chemicals, is harming the world's soil. An example of such a company is Monsanto, which makes substances for farmers to kill insects and weeds. Monsanto is also one of the biggest companies selling GMO seeds to farmers around the world. At least partly as a result of Shiva's efforts, the Indian government has been hesitant to approve genetically modified crops for food.

CONTROVERSY

Although Vandana Shiva is respected around the world for her food activism, some people say she makes wild, untrue claims to support her arguments. For instance, she claims large seed companies have caused the suicides of thousands of Indian farmers who have lost their farms. Many of her supporters repeat this statement as evidence of the damage caused by large-scale farming. But in fact, researchers have shown that the rate of suicide among Indian farmers, while high, has not grown since the introduction of big-business farms and genetically modified seeds.

One of the modified crops Shiva and her organization oppose is called golden rice. This variety of rice has been modified by adding vitamin A. Many claim that putting this additive in rice will improve the health of millions of poor children in India and the rest of the

Golden rice *(right)* is a genetically modified food. The rice has added vitamin A, which gives it a golden color in comparison to white rice *(left)*.

world, who don't normally get enough vitamin A. But Shiva believes those children would be better off if they had access to vegetables traditionally farmed in India. Those vegetables have natural vitamin A, which Shiva says is more nutritious than the vitamin added to golden rice. She believes big businesses promote golden rice because they can make money from it, not because it is the best nutrition for people.

To help raise awareness for her campaign against big-business farming and genetically modified crops, Shiva traveled across southern Europe in spring 2014. She traveled to Greece, Italy, and France, where she celebrated International Seed Day. At every stop on her journey, she was greeted by fans who thanked her for standing up for small farmers against big agriculture.

RACHEL PARENT
SPREADING AWARENESS OF GMOS

Rachel Parent remembers the first time she heard of a GMO. She was ten years old and eating cereal for breakfast, when her grandmother pointed out that the cereal may have GMOs in it. She didn't think much of the comment at the time, but the idea was planted in her mind. Later, she said, "The thought of GMOs really stayed in my head and a couple years later, having to do a speech for school, I wanted to do something that would really impact a lot of people and how they really lived their lives."

Rachel Parent in 2014

Rachel's school speech on GMOs was well received. But even more importantly, she uncovered a love of activism. While researching for her speech, she realized just how much of an effect GMOs could have on all forms of life. And she was shocked to learn that food companies weren't required to identify GMOs on their labels. She recalls: "I was confused and angry. I'll never forget when my world was turned upside down. I learned I was part of a big science experiment. I couldn't believe that our government wasn't doing any independent testing on the long-term effects of GMOs on our health and the environment."

Rachel realized she wanted to help spread awareness about GMOs. More importantly, she wanted to press for mandatory labeling by food companies. "This isn't a matter of whether you want GMOs or not. This is a matter of freedom of choice and our right to know," she explained. So that year, when she was twelve, Rachel founded her own nonprofit group, Kids Right to Know. Its mission is to educate youth about health and environmental concerns, with a focus on genetically modified food and the need for proper testing and labeling.

Through Kids Right to Know, Rachel has worked to raise awareness in Canada, the United States, and other parts of the world. She organized a GMO Kids Right to Know rally in Toronto. The video of her speech became a hot YouTube view. She's attended many health- and food-related events, given many presentations, and even traveled to Brazil's Amazon rain forest. Rachel has become skilled at answering people's questions about why she believes that mandatory labeling of GMOs is the least the government should do to protect people's health. She's gotten used to responding to people who don't agree with her.

So when popular Canadian cable news host Kevin O'Leary called anti-GMO activists "stupid," Rachel couldn't help replying. In May 2013,

Without a label, there's no way to tell GMO foods apart from other foods.

Activists gather for a March against Monsanto in Toronto in 2013.

nearly two million protesters around the world joined in a March against Monsanto to protest the large producer of genetically modified food. Discussing the protest, O'Leary said, "You're an ignorant person if you get a placard and you walk around the street saying 'What Monsanto does is bad for human beings.' You're just stupid."

Rachel responded, "I want to respond to Mr. Kevin O'Leary's . . . statement about 'stupid' people who protest against Monsanto. I challenge you, Mr. O'Leary, to have me on your show next week, and if you promise not to use the word *stupid*, then I won't use the word *fascist*." O'Leary accepted Rachel's challenge, and Rachel did appear on his show. She used the opportunity to inform his viewers that it's impossible to know if GMOs are safe, since there have never been long-term safety tests. And she even got O'Leary to admit, "We're in a long-term study— you're eating genetically modified food whether you like it or not."

The appearance on O'Leary's show earned Rachel new followers, and she continues to spread the word about the potential dangers of GMOs. In her spare time, she works in her organic garden; enjoys horseback riding; and works at an animal sanctuary rescue camp, where she helps care for tigers, monkeys, and lemurs.

MICHAEL POLLAN
WRITING ABOUT FOOD'S ORIGINS

Michael Pollan is known as one of the world's most important activists for ethical eating. Through his books and speeches, he has gotten people to think about where their food comes from—and what the consequences of that journey are. But when he was a kid in the 1960s, he loved Pop-Tarts, packaged meals, chocolate cakes called Yodels, and lots of other junk food. In that way, he was just like most other kids of his time.

One way Pollan was different from other kids was his love of gardening. As a boy, he spent time in his grandpa's huge garden. When he grew older, he started his own garden in his yard in Long Island. "I only grew stuff that you could eat," he said. "I didn't see the point of anything else. I grew peppers, and melons, and strawberries."

Michael Pollan in 2013

That's where his interest in food was born. But Pollan also loved learning. That's why he became a journalist. He didn't have to be an expert on the things he wrote about. He only had to tell the story of what he learned. He began his career working for magazines, and he published his first book, about gardening, in 1991. But it wasn't until 2002 that his work started to really change the world. That's when he published an article called "Power Steer" in the *New York Times Magazine*.

Pollan wanted to learn about beef—where people got it, how it was raised and sold, and how it affected our health. So he bought a steer. In following the steer's existence all the way to its place as meat in the supermarket, he learned a lot. Traditionally raised cattle are pumped full of antibiotics that might not be good for people. Cattle, which naturally feed on grass, have their diets altered so they eat mostly corn. Sometimes they also eat cow blood and chicken poop.

The article got a lot of attention. Suddenly, consumers were asking where their beef came from. Demand for grass-fed beef went up. Chefs started serving grass-fed beef in their restaurants. And "Power Steer" became the centerpiece of Pollan's book, *The Omnivore's Dilemma*. In this book, Pollan eats four meals and traces each meal back to its origins. A McDonald's lunch, for

Pollan's book, *The Omnivore's Dilemma*, was published in 2006.

example, begins in an Iowa cornfield. Corn is used to feed the cows that eventually become beef. Corn makes up the oil that the fries are cooked in. Corn is turned into high-fructose corn syrup, which sweetens the sodas.

The book was a wake-up call for people to pay more attention to where their food was coming from. Since *The Omnivore's Dilemma,* Pollan has published four more books about food and eating, including *Food Rules: An Eater's Manual.*

One reason Pollan has been so effective in getting his message out is that he's not too strict. He still eats meat—just not meat that's been raised on antibiotics and corn. "I didn't want to become a vegetarian," he said. People like his education-based approach: be informed about what you eat. His philosophy can be summed up in seven words, which form the basis for another of his books, *In Defense of Food.* "Eat food. Not too much. Mostly plants."

WHAT CAN *YOU* DO?

Environmental activists come in all ages, races, and nationalities. They have a wide variety of interests, skills, and talents. So what exactly do they have in common? They each noticed a problem, and they took action. Whether the problem that attracted their attention was related to food, climate change, or another environmental issue, they all became activists because they realized they wanted to make a change in their world.

You don't have to be a particular type of person to be an activist. You don't have to start your own nonprofit organization, travel around the world, or get invited to give a TED Talk. You just need to commit to doing something to make a change.

Your change can include a small change to your own habits, such as committing to picking up trash in your neighborhood or using as little electricity as you can for one week. You can spread the word to your family, your friends, your neighbors, and others in your school or community.

For example, maybe you commit to using less water. That project might begin with setting a timer for showers. Or you might work with your family to install water-reducing faucets in your home. Those are individual actions. But to be an activist, you might spread the word about your efforts by starting a blog to write about the changes you make and how they affect your life and the lives of those around you. Share your blog with classmates and adults such as teachers who might be interested.

You can also write letters to politicians or to a newspaper or website. Their addresses (for e-mail and for physical delivery) are easy to find online. Politicians are usually eager to hear from local people like you. Tell them about changes you have made and changes you would like to see. Another idea is to make your own videos to post on YouTube. Use a smartphone or portable video camera to record stories you make up, document things you notice in your environment, or even interview people such as other activists—adults *and* kids.

You can try some or all of these ideas. You can pick the ones that fit your personality and skills the best. Give it a try . . . you just might find that the activist life is for you!

Source Notes

7   Sindya N. Bhanoo, "Artist, 11, Campaigns to Save Gulf Birds," *New York Times,* June 15, 2010, http://green.blogs.nytimes.com/2010/06/15/artist-11 -campaigns-to-save-gulf-birds/?_r=0.

9   Ella Van Cleave, "TEDxYouth@Victoria—Ella Van Cleave—Save the Dolphin Smile,"YouTube video, 11:12, posted by "TEDx Talks," January 12, 2012, http://www.youtube.com/watch?v=-FKbUp65XrI.

9   Melissa Cronin, "Meet the 16-Year-Old Activist Who's Leading the Fight to Free Captive Orcas," *The Dodo,* July 29, 2014, https://www.thedodo.com /meet-the-16-year-old-activist--647475701.html.

10   Van Cleave, "TEDxYouth@Victoria."

10   Cronin, "Meet the 16-Year-Old Activist."

12   Jenny Inglee, "A Conversation with Jane Goodall, the World's Most Influential Animal Activist," *TakePart,* September 26, 2001, http://www.takepart.com /article/2011/09/26/jane-goodall.

12   "Study Corner: Biography," Jane Goodall Institute, accessed September 10, 2015, http://archive1.janegoodall.org/study-corner-biography.

14   Inglee, "A Conversation with Jane Goodall."

16   "Alec Loorz," iMatter, accessed September 3, 2015, http://www.imatteryouth .org/#!alec-loorz/c8c1.

17–18   Ibid.

18   "Our Mission," The Climate Reality Project, accessed September 3, 2015, https://www.climaterealityproject.org/our-mission.

19   Anna Rose Mohr-Almeida, "March Member of the Month: Anna Rose Mohr-Almeida," iMatter, March 3, 2015, http://www.imatteryouth.org /march-member-of-the-month-anna-rose-mohr-almeida/.

20   "Voices of the March: Jimmy Betts as 'Anna Rose Mohr-Almeida,'" YouTube video, 5:15, posted by "Gavain UPrichard," November 6, 2014, https://www .youtube.com/watch?v=RgWonnikNsc.

20   Ibid.

21   Mohr-Almeida, "March Member of the Month."

21   Ibid.

22   Nic Maclellan, "Young Pacific Islanders Are Not Climate Change Victims—
      They're Fighting," *Guardian* (Manchester), September 21, 2014, http://www
      .theguardian.com/commentisfree/2014/sep/22/young-pacific-islanders-are
      -not-climate-change-victims-theyre-fighting.

22   Ibid.

23   Ibid.

24   Xiuhtezcatl Roske-Martinez, "Xiuhtezcatl Fighting for the Survival of His
      Generation," YouTube video, 6:05, posted by "Earth Guardians," May 21,
      2012, https://www.youtube.com/watch?v=b6PrMybQzyQ.

25–26 Xiuhtezcatl Roske-Martinez, "Wisdom from Xiuhtezcatl, a 13 Year Old
      Indigenous Environmental Activist," YouTube video, 8:09, posted by "Earth
      Guardians," February 1, 2014, https://www.youtube.com/watch?v=-
      CMoJ0MjzVE.

26   Xiuhtezcatl Roske-Martinez, "What the Frack? Music Video by the Earth
      Guardians," YouTube video, 5:23, posted by "Earth Guardians," November 15,
      2013, https://www.youtube.com/watch?v=JxI7ERflFfM.

27–28 Clare Thompson, "Meet the Woman Who Shut Down Chicago's Dirty Coal
      Plants," *Grist,* April 15, 2013, http://grist.org/climate-energy/interview
      -wkimberly-wasserman-nieto-goldman-prize-winner/.

28   Ibid.

29   Ibid.

31   Michael Specter, "Seeds of Doubt," *New Yorker,* August 25, 2014, http://www
      .newyorker.com/magazine/2014/08/25/seeds-of-doubt.

34   Allison Vuchnich and Erica Vella, "Meet Rachel Parent—the Teen Fighting for
      GMO Labelling in Canada." *Global News* (Canada), October 6, 2014, http://
      globalnews.ca/news/1600441/meet-rachel-parent-the-teen-fighting-for
      -gmo-labelling-in-canada/.

34   "A Note from Rachel," Kids Right to Know, accessed September 3, 2015,
      http://www.kidsrighttoknow.com/a-note-from-rachel/.

35   Vuchnich and Vella, "Meet Rachel Parent."

36   Kevin O'Leary, "The Big 3," *CBC* Player, May 27, 2013, http://www.cbc.ca
        /player/News/TV+Shows/Lang+&+O'Leary+Exchange/ID/2387888169/.

36   Ethan A. Huff, "Fourteen-Year-Old GMO Protester and Activist Annihilates
        Bullying TV Host," Natural News, August 18, 2013, http://www
        .naturalnews.com/041670_GMO_protestor_TV_host_Rachel_Parent
        .html#ixzz3Ukq1gdSJ.

37   Michael Pollan, "In Conversation: Michael Pollan and Adam Platt," *New York
        Magazine,* April 16, 2013, http://michaelpollan.com/interviews/in
        -conversation-michael-pollan-and-adam-platt/.

39   Ibid.

Glossary

advocate: to support or argue for an idea or a plan

asthma: a lung disease that makes it difficult for people to breathe

climate change: a change in global weather patterns caused by human activity

genetically modified organism (GMO): any living organism whose genes have been artificially changed

global warming: the gradual increase in Earth's temperatures that scientists attribute to human activities

indigenous: native to a particular place. Indigenous people are generally considered to be the first group of people who lived in an area.

organic farming: a style of agriculture that does not use artificial pesticides or other human-made chemicals, but instead relies on crop rotation, manure, and other natural aids

renewable energy: power from resources that are naturally replenished, such as sunlight, wind, rain, or tides

shale: a layered rock made of clay or mud and other minerals

Selected Bibliography

Inglee, Jenny. "A Conversation with Jane Goodall, the World's Most Influential Animal Activist." *TakePart,* September 26, 2011. http://www.takepart.com/article/2011/09/26/jane-goodall.

"Kimberly Wasserman." The Goldman Environmental Prize. Accessed September 3, 2015. http://www.goldmanprize.org/recipient/kimberly-wasserman.

Maclellan, Nic. "Young Pacific Islanders Are Not Climate Change Victims—They're Fighting." *Guardian* (Manchester), September 21, 2014. http://www.theguardian.com/commentisfree/2014/sep/22/young-pacific-islanders-are-not-climate-change-victims-theyre-fighting.

Martin, Claire. "Xiuhtezcatl Roske-Martinez, 14, Wants to Save the World." *Denver Post,* May 28, 2014. http://www.denverpost.com/lifestyles/ci_25852604/xiuhtezcatl-roske-martinez-boulder-middle-school-student-has.

Vuchnich, Allison, and Erica Vella. "Meet Rachel Parent—the Teen Fighting for GMO Labelling in Canada." *Global News* (Canada), October 6, 2014. http://globalnews.ca/news/1600441/meet-rachel-parent-the-teen-fighting-for-gmo-labelling-in-canada/.

Further Information

Bouler, Olivia. *Olivia's Birds: Saving the Gulf.* New York: Sterling Children's Books, 2011. See Olivia's illustrations and read descriptions of common and not-so-common gulf birds.

Braun, Eric. *Taking Action for Civil and Political Rights.* Minneapolis: Lerner Publications, 2017. Meet real-life activists making a difference in the world of politics, civil rights, and social change.

iMatter: Kids vs. Global Warming
http://www.imatteryouth.org
Learn more about global warming and what you can do to get involved on Alec Loorz's iMatter website.

Kids Right to Know
http://www.kidsrighttoknow.com
Visit the site of Rachel Parent's nonprofit organization, which focuses on health and environmental concerns—and especially the potential dangers of GMOs.

McCarthy, Pat. *Friends of the Earth: A History of American Environmentalism.* Chicago: Chicago Review Press, 2013. Get the scoop on ten of the earliest American environmental activists.

A Student's Guide to Global Climate Change
http://epa.gov/climatechange/kids/index.html
Visit this site to learn the basics about climate change and get ideas for how you can be part of the solution.

TakingITGlobal: Youth Media
https://www.tigweb.org/youth-media
Find worldwide platforms for sharing your art, writing, and opinions at this site.

Index

Photo Acknowledgments

The images in this book are used with the permission of: © panki/Shutterstock.com (sunburst backgrounds); © CataVic/Shutterstock.com, p. 3 (people); © venimo/ Shutterstock.com (megaphone); © photka/Shutterstock.com, p. 4 (left); © paintings/ Shutterstock.com, p. 4 (right); © Evgenia Bolyukh/Shutterstock.com, p. 5; © Charles Eshelman/FilmMagic/Getty Images, p. 6; © Win McNamee/Getty Images, p. 7; Courtesy Olivia Bouler, p. 8; © iStockphoto.com/ShinOkamoto, p. 9; Sara Gouveia Africapictures.net/Newscom, p. 10; © Barcroft Media/Getty Images, p. 11; © Pablo Blazquez Dominguez/Getty Images, p. 12; © Bettmann/Corbis, p. 13; © Duffy-Marie Arnoult/WireImage/Getty Images, p. 14; Giulio Marcocchi/Sipa Press./Sanity_ gm.020/1010312212/Newscom, p. 16; AP Photo/Mark Humphrey, p. 17; REUTERS/ Samantha Sais, p. 19; UPI/John Angelillo/Newscom, p. 21; ©Timothy A. Clary/Getty Images, p. 22; © Reinhard Dirscherl/WaterFrame RF/Getty Images, p. 23; Courtesy of Earth Guardians, p. 24; AP Photo/David Zalubowski, p. 25; Courtesy Goldman Environmental Prize Materials, p. 27; © Amanda Rivkin/Corbis, p. 28; ©Amanda Edwards/WireImage/Getty Images, p. 30; © Hemis/Alamy, p. 31; Courtesy Kids Right To Know, p. 34; © iStockphoto.com/baona, p. 35; © Dawn Lioutas/Dreamstime. com, p. 36; © Jeff Morgan 11/Alamy, p. 37; © Bill Hogan/Chicago Tribune/MCT via Getty Images, p. 38.

Front cover: © iStockphoto.com/billnoll (dot background); © Milos Djapovic/ Shutterstock.com (grunge frame) © Vertyr/Shutterstock.com (forest); © panki/ Shutterstock.com (sunburst background).